A Box of Comfits

The Alchemy Spoon
2023 Pamphlet Competition Anthology

Clayhanger Press

Newcastle-under-Lyme & Douglas, Isle of Man

This book or any portion thereof may not be reproduced or used in any manner whatsoever without the express written permission of the copyright holders except for the use of brief quotations in a book review. Copyright of all the poems remains with the authors who assert their rights.

First Printing, 2024

Published by Clayhanger Press

All rights reserved.

ISBN-978-1-917017-00-8

ACKNOWLEDGEMENTS

In 2023 *The Alchemy Spoon* invited submissions to a pamphlet competition, this anthology contains selected poems from those entrants whose anonymised pamphlet submissions were chosen by the judge Chris Hardy for longlisting, those whose entries were shortlisted and a poem from the winner Ann Craig whose pamphlet *Ordinary Magic* will be published by Clayhanger Press in 2024.

The editors of *The Alchemy Spoon* are grateful to Chris Hardy for his diligence and attention to detail in judging the competition and for writing his insightful report.

The following poems in the Anthology have previously been published.

'When I came to visit you at home' was first published in the NHS anthology 'These are the Hands', Fair Acre Press 2020.

A version of 'Some data and a little insight' was first published by *Ink Sweat & Tears*, 2016.

'Going Home' won second prize and was published online by Grey Hen Press, 2021. https://www.greyhenpress.com/results-2021/

'The Boy, Trevor' was first published in *Washed with Noon*. Vole Books Summer Anthology, 2023.

'2001 Fuchsia Rose' was first published in *Twyckenham Notes* Issue 15, Spring 2022.

'Ilaria Triptych' was runner up in the 2021 Poetry on the Lake Wyvern Competition.

Cover image:

Structure of sulphamic acid. A soluble chemical, that exists as small white crystals when solid – reactions with which are often used in the manufacture of artificial sweeteners. *

*Gwyneth Thurgood, 'sulphamic acid': (Wellcome Collection). Licence 4.0 International (CC BY 4.0). https://wellcomecollection.org/works/kecjy7ev

A Box of Comfits

At last the Dodo said, 'Everybody has won, and all must have prizes.' 'But who is to give the prizes?' quite a chorus of voices asked. 'Why, she, of course,' said the Dodo, pointing to Alice with one finger; and the whole party at once crowded round her, calling out in a confused way, 'Prizes! Prizes!' Alice had no idea what to do, and in despair she put her hand in her pocket, and pulled out a box of comfits, (luckily the salt water had not got into it), and handed them round as prizes. There was exactly one a-piece all round.

Lewis Carroll *Alice's Adventures in Wonderland* (1865)

Contents

Acknowledgements		3
Contents		8
Judge's Report		10
The Poems		17
World Made Magic	Ann Craig	18
2001 Fuchsia Rose	Julie Runacres	20
Going Home	Judith Wozniak	21
The Boy, Trevor	Judith Wozniak	22
Ilaria Triptych	Sharon Ashton	23
To the nurse who said I should never have a child	Sarah Drury	25
Confined to bed with smallpox	Laura Stanley	26
When I came to visit you at home	Neil Douglas	27
Toyah Willcox and Robert Fripp cover 'Heroes' in lockdown on VE day	Veronica Zundel	28
Some data and a little insight	Oliver Comins	30
The Spectacular Spinning Songbook Tour, 2011	Louise Walker	31
The Goose Mother	Zoë Green	32
Student Teacher	Penny Shutt	33
The Road	John Martin	34

Death Notice	Michael Klimeš	36
Grandad keeps pigeons and canaries	Kathryn Anna Marshall	37
Petsamo	Morag Smith	38
Every time I come here, I wish that I could leave	Emily Fox	40

The Poets 44

Judge's Report

General comments on what I look for when reading poems:

'The best words in the best order'. Samuel Coleridge 1827
'No ideas but in things'. William Carlos Williams 1927

The poet should have something to say along with the skill to reveal it. A poem should feel to the reader as if it were essential and necessary for the writer and at some point display awareness of how strange the ordinary and every-day is. Other key features are:

- Close attention when describing things – making the reader see them new.
- The use of words which are cut and fit to meaning and emotion – are accurate, precise, concise.
- Poems might be intrinsically difficult, but the poet shouldn't make them difficult on purpose.
- Saying, 'This happened and I feel anguished or ecstatic about it', isn't interesting or informative, in poetry at least – a speech in a drama, or novel, is different.
- No matter how urgent, desperate, tragic, joyful the subject of a poem is, the poet should make a poem not a statement, essay or polemic.
- All emotions, from adoration to hate, are acceptable in poetry but they must be used by and not have control over, the poet. Poems should be open to the reader's imagination, experience and interpretation.

The submissions to the Alchemy Spoon Poetry Pamphlet Competition 2023 had a number of main themes:

- The resilience and central strength of women in communities and families.
- Time and life, passing, seized and lost.
- Physical and mental suffering.
- Family memories.
- Community and culture.

- Teachers and pupils.
- Love and desire.
- The Cosmos.
- Threatened Nature.

Considerations when assessing a pamphlet – a group of poems rather than single poems.

There was no requirement for a thematic or style connection within the group submitted but with only 8 – 10 poems in each submission I looked for entries where there were few weak points, such as poems that are not as carefully phrased and / or powerful as the others in the set. From all the entries, I selected a long list of eighteen.

2000 Cerulean	Julie Runacres
A Pill of Light	Laura Stanley
As I was saying	John Martin
A Study of Drowning	Emily Fox
Cwtch	Judith Wozniak
Dancing with Eve	Sharon Ashton
Empathy for the Devil	Neil Douglas
Leavers Ball	Penny Shutt
Love carries the future	Michael Klimeš
Making Dolmades in Essex	Judith Wozniak
Minus	Veronica Zundel
Ordinary Magic	Ann Craig
Photo Album	Louise Walker
Sectioned with a pen	Sarah Drury
Shadow Child	Zoë Green
Someone not a stranger	Oliver Comins
The daughter of a man who loved birds	Kathryn Marshall
Weft	Morag Smith

I was very aware of how important the collections were to the poets: how much care, thought, concentration, and emotion had gone into the poems. All of those on the long list had their particular merits but I wish to comment on six of them that I felt deserved particular mention.

A Pill of Light: A well-focused set of poems with a strong theme, resurrecting the life of a formidable, self-sacrificing woman, Dorothy Pattison, 'Dora', a Nun and innovative Nurse in 19th century Walsall. These poems bring back someone who should never have been forgotten.

A Study of Drowning: vivid accounts of dealing with physical suffering, a strange and disturbed, aged parent who dies, and a loving husband. 'Chronic Pain as an Unwelcome Caller' ironically and bravely confronts suffering as a murderer at the door, 'I am prepared for all eventualities/ have been ready for the assailant my/ whole life ...'

Empathy for the Devil: written from the point of view of a medical practitioner. The poems use case work to portray the Devil's Work in a city – the struggles of human beings to stay alive, free of pain, doing right; and what a doctor must try and fail to do, and the demands that makes.

Love carries the future: spare, beautiful poems about the family rituals performed when a beloved grandmother, 'Babi', dies. The poems are a lament, also a celebration of how a Czech family survived, nurtured itself and each member over many decades, across many countries, through love and care for each other.

Minus: a tribute to a Jewish family, descendants of the Holocaust dead and of those who survived the pogroms, to struggle and survive in wartime England, expressing anguish for what the genocide did to memory, lives; whole nations and continents poisoned for ever. And a furious refusal to forgive.

The daughter of a man who loved birds: a sequence with a uniform style, no titles, broken phrasing and lineation, generating a sense of agitation and fear. A frightened, threatened, girl growing up, who later finds herself in an unhappy, confining marriage. Effective use of dialect in places to fix the poems in place and time.

It was fairly straightforward to reduce the entries to the 18 on the long list. Selecting the short list and especially the winner was more difficult. The five in the short list are, in their own ways, as 'good' as each other and could each have won. They all have something to say and know how they wish to say it, with a clear understanding that poetry is a way of using language distinct from other forms of writing.

THE SHORT LIST:

2000 Cerulean	Julie Runacres
Cwtch	Judith Wozniak
Dancing with Eve	Sharon Ashton
Making Dolmades in Essex	Judith Wozniak
Ordinary Magic	Ann Craig

Highly Commended

2000 Cerulean: each year the Pantone Colour Institute, a manufacturer of paint, announces a 'colour of the year'. This declaration is deployed at the start of each of a remarkable and ambitious series of 10 prose poems. The poems are intense, clever and controlled. Together they are a commentary, using fashion – the world of luxurious decoration and affluence – on how this superficial aspect of life co-exists alongside, in fact depends on and yet avoids, the poverty, oppression, and lethal violence that our way of life creates. Firstly the colour of the chosen year is described, in the language of the manufacturer, for example: 2001 Fuchsia Rose. 'A bright, feel-good feminine colour ... passionate, intense and exciting'. Then follows a powerfully constructed prose poem about the attack on the Twin Towers: 'journalist Conor O'Clery spies man, 30's, clinging to a window strut on north tower, 90+ floors up waving ... looks like his shirt'. The intention is to contrast the banality of the advertising with what actually happened in one of the centres of advertising that year.

Commended

Cwtch: a distinct sense of place and culture – Wales ('Cwtch' – a cubby hole) – some time ago. Growing up on the farm, seaside resorts, and a forgotten way of life:

> 'They whisper Welsh in the scullery. Alone in the best room I
> kick the oak chair leg in time with the grandfather clock and
> try not to look at the picture over the red-brick hearth' (Capel Salem)

The poems radiate a warm, affectionate longing for a secure, family past, inescapably lost to time and change. And the endeavour is also to let the lost voices of the ordinary people be heard:

> 'All that's left is the castle keep, a still pool of water
> and the sound of a bell that tolls before a storm
> for the silenced voices under the shifting sand'. (Kenfig)

Dancing with Eve: women and womanhood, being a woman with other women, girls and men. This underlying theme is presented through the lives of women and daughters, mythic female beings – Circe, Eve – and historic figures. There are two especially strong, longer poems. One concerns Queen Elizabeth I, the other Ilaria del Carretto, (1379 – 1405), second wife of an Italian Lord. Her story tells of the lonely plight of girls taken to men and given to them in marriage, unready, subservient, unwilling,

> 'To endure all that my mother told me must be endured,
> I take flight. Upwards, upwards, upwards I soar
> to the frescoed ceiling above my husband's bed'. (Blue)

The collection ends with 'Portrait of Molly in Three Lipsticks', three poems in which a daughter watches and also remembers her mother. The language and phrasing used is lively, impassioned, rich, cumulative, also sparse, spare and always suited to what the writer feels must be said.

Making Dolmades in Essex: a child of a single, sad, mother in Essex is befriended by a Greek family, 'with a Dad', who move in next door.

> 'I peek at them through a spy-hole
> in the fence. Conker-haired children,
> freckled with gold dust, play that game
> I liked best – walking on his shiny shoes
> in their socks..' (Other People's Families)

A vivid sense of community in suburbia, warm-hearted, affectionate and domestic: how ordinary life – neighbours, friends, youthful romance, going to a show, sweets and cakes – goes on all the time as a cloak or mask concealing, and revealing, the deepest needs and emotions.

All these superb submissions deserve to win this prize. But as in a race or a cup final someone has to win, even if the teams are equal.

THE WINNER OF THE ALCHEMY SPOON POETRY PAMPHLET COMPETITION, 2023.

ORDINARY MAGIC
by
Ann Craig

Ordinary Magic: an innovative set of poems making skilful use of Scots, honouring a mother who has 'ordinary magic', which is the power and knowledge to bring up children in a hard, proud, confident, working class environment and despite everything spread happiness and comfort. The poems are like a rich, slow-cooked pie or stew:

> '.. that big pot o rabbit stew,
> bubblin, simmerin awa, waarmin,
> mammy whisperin in her ear,
> made wae luv fur a dark day.' (The Cauldron)

The sequence commences with a son or daughter saying farewell by cleaning the house of every speck left by the departed practitioner of 'ordinary magic'. There follow poems showing that the mother is intent on making her children see how the world is a sort of heaven, as well as making it so for them. The final poem, about an old man, is sorrowing and brave: the dialect carefully spelled out to portray not just a man but also, through the precision of the phrasing, a distinct sense of sadness, loss and of how a cultural unit – a community – sustains itself and its members through everything we all have to face.

Ann will work with Alchemy Spoon Editor Vanessa Lampert to expand the submission to a pamphlet length manuscript for publication by Clayhanger Press in 2024.

Chris Hardy
Competition Judge

The Poems

World Made Magic

She walks you to the nearest green space,
Busses are fur folk who canny use their legs hen.
After miles, she covers your eyes,
Noo pet, when ye open yer wee een,
soak up aw the magic o this fairy den.
They're only lettin us in cos it's the furst day o spring.

A banquet of snowdrops, crocuses, bluebells,
dandelion clocks drifting in the slanting light,
new yellow gorse, pigeon's secret coos.
In heaven, you eat jam pieces, and chocolate buttons.
She crowns you with daisy chains.

Ma ain wee fairy queen.
Look at that sky wee wummin,
it's like sumbody's lit a thoosand candles
it's enough tae gie ye religion.

Jist when ye think the wurld's too dark
tae fathom, the light cums back.
We've goat tae look efter it aw though,
we've only goat wan wurld, it's up tae us.

Like conspirators, she tells you
of mountains with secrets caves,
great rivers with magical beasts,
enchanted forests full of elves.
It's all wonderment.
Smells of warm earth, cool winds,
cooriein down beside the big tree,

This is my wean mister tree, she's
cum tae say hello, the branches rustle,
oh ah ken she's bonnie, takes efter her mammy,
dinnae worry ah've telt her aboot the growin things.

The road back seems longer,
peppered with treats, ice cream, jelly babies.
The last part hazy, being carried close
in that golden sunset down grey streets.

Clothes come off. A damp sponge
wipes sticky hands and wind slapped face.
Gentle kisses on your nose, eyes closed.
The *allowed* bunch of wild flowers
in a jam jar beside the bed.
That lingering smell of honey gorse, and her.

Ann Craig

PANTONE®
17-2031 TPX
Fuchsia Rose

2001 PANTONE 17-2031 Fuchsia Rose. A bright, feel-good feminine colour, Fuchsia Rose is passionate, intense and exciting.

Unreal. Shining city on a hill. Falling towers. Mental videotape on perpetual loop. Through military binoculars, journalist Conor O'Clery spies man, 30s, clinging to a window strut on north tower, 90+ floors up, waving white cloth — looks like his shirt — soundless shapes descend in air — arms outstretched in crucifixion. It's like 10 seconds down to Vesey, flesh atomised like pollen. John Malley, firefighter FDNY, steps through revolving doors of 7, thinks what the hell? this force that's going on, must be concussion from some explosion, turns out it's down pressure wind of 110 storeys beginning their imploding. When the building pops an orange flash a strap of fire and pops again like every floor goes chu-chu-chu and pancakes down. Can't see up, can't see back, can't outrun it, it's like it just keeps on coming piling up and up, loads of cementation, powdery insulation, a blizzard with metal whatever-you-call-it in it. He guesses this is what it's like to be dead and not sure he isn't, all full of the cloud, they're all eating the cloud, whatever it's like, very thick not-smoke, it's like everything, like a sandstorm and so silent now it's down, before the Maydays start and the guys all screaming. Now he's looking at the sound. Looks up, and it looks like a ticker tape parade with all this stuff starts coming down, a piece of keyboard not four-inch square.

Julie Runacres

Notes on sources
O'Clery, Conor. 'Eyewitness to 9/11- When Hell Came Calling.' IrishCentral.com, 9 Sept. 2022, www.irishcentral.com/opinion/others/eyewitness-911-hell.
Macqueen, Graeme. Volume 2 118 Witnesses: The Firefighters' Testimony to Explosions in the Twin Towers. (2006).

Going Home

Her bus wheezes up the hill past Pisgah Chapel
where her mother played the organ each Sunday.
Sooty terraced houses lean together like bad teeth.

She sees Trefor the butcher closing for the day,
setting out sluiced trays with a fresh ruff of paper,
Elias Funerals with their display of dusty flowers.

On the corner outside the Co-op, Howard Marks,
down from Oxford, smokes rollups with bad boys
from the Comp, turning heads with his long hair.

Children spill from *The Fish Plaice* in Moriah Street
clutching Friday night bags of scraps and chips,
licking greasy fingers slid out from mittens.

Once they pass Langford's Dairy the driver slows
to drop her off, between stops, at the Top Cross.
She remembers teaching him at Marlas Infants.

She skirts the puddles in the lane to her cottage,
unpacks her basket; salty cockles, laverbread
from Bridgend market. Treats for her daughter

home from London for the weekend.
There's time to heat the bakestone for Welsh cakes
before Willy Pentre delivers fresh eggs and…

Did you have a good snooze Gwen? A girl
in a plastic apron is kneeling by her chair
rubbing her arm. She keeps her eyes closed.

Gwen is not her name, she's Gwyneth Dilys
and they have put her in the wrong clothes.
Her daughter will be coming soon to take her home.

Judith Wozniak

The Boy, Trevor

I watch our neighbours from my bedroom.
Trevor kicks his football against the wall, *thud*

thud, until his mum raps on the window
clattering her rings against the glass.

His dad mows the grass up and down in stripes.
The mum appears with a basket of washing,

pegs fanned between her teeth, hair hidden
under a chiffon scarf, one roller peeping out

under the knot at the front. Trevor shows off,
if he knows I'm looking, doing his Charlie Chaplin

impression, twirling a garden cane he's pinched
from the wigwam holding up their runner beans

or cartwheels across the grass, so his shorts slip
down enough to flash the pale hull of his hips.

I'm revising, listening to *Downtown* on a loop.
When it's dark he'll climb the apple tree

at the bottom of the garden, call out *cuckoo,
cuckoo*, until I turn on my light.

Judith Wozniak

Ilaria Triptych

Ilaria del Carretto (1379 – 1405) the second wife of Paolo Guinigi, Lord of Lucca, died in childbirth. Her tomb in the cathedral at Lucca has never held her body.

Blue
To endure all that my mother told me must be endured, I take flight.
Upwards, upwards, upwards I soar
to the frescoed ceiling above my husband's bed,
hovering beneath winter, spring, summer and autumn
before swooping and forcing myself between birds
that gather in blossoms of white and saffron,
calling down to my marble self from citrus-sweet air:
Remember, Ilaria, remember the moment everything changed.
And when the moment comes, it is suffused with blue,
not the boasting lapis of my husband's house,
but the watery blue of a morning sky above Liguria
as it clashes with mauve fringes of alpine snowbells;
the black-rimmed blue I saw once in the eyes
of a wolf tracked down and caged by my father;
the strawberry-rippled blue above my mother's garden
that evening they found me and said the time had come.

Childbirth
The corridors that separate me from men whisper:
Hush, take off your shoes, the lady is sleeping
but the child lies on my heart, I cannot sleep.
Close the casements gently, her breathing is soft
but the child lies on my lungs, I cannot breathe.
When the lady wakes, perhaps she will eat
but the child lies on my stomach, I cannot eat.
Only when I am safely delivered will I eat;
I will eat almond pastries and apples wrapped
in soft cheese dough from my mother's majolica dish
She talks of her dead mother! Pray it is not the fever
the gold-rimmed dish painted with Our Lady
enfolding sweet Jesus in her dress of blue.
I have prayed to Our Lady and Juno Lucina.
I have worn the rank marten pelt against my skin.
I have made myself invisible in my husband's house.

After death

In transept-dim light they dance about my tomb,
some interested only in the dog at my feet—
a dog for a faithful body, but what choice did we have,
Maria before me, Piacentina and Jacopa after?
We were merely land for Lucca to sow and harvest,
our days measured with child, or not with child.
And now attendants scold these scurrying children:
Shush! Shush! The beautiful lady sleeps!
But they cannot wake me; I do not lie here.

Sharon Ashton

To the nurse who said I should never have a child

The room a crypt, my gown a sterile rag,
your words a serpent twisted like a noose.
I am a mermaid, washed up on shingle shore,
carrageen shrouds my ashen face.

Sailors husk my iridescent scales,
they shout, 'Sexy legs! Psychotic whore!',
then toss my womb – barnacles encrust
placenta, staining Indian Ocean currents.

I rise, a lunatic; silent, medicated,
thrashing like a bird encased in steel:
Angel of the North. I mutilate
my clitoris with Lalique glass I can't afford.

My hands clutch remnants of an embryo,
my uterus imbrued beneath blood moon.

Sarah Drury

Confined to Bed with Smallpox

*From a sequence of poems about Sister Dora,
a nurse who lived and worked in Walsall, West Midlands
from 1865 to 1878*

At first, she is a shadow behind a curtain.
No one knows who she is,
this newcomer, stranger, outsider.
Like spores, rumours grow

and thicken through the streets.
The locals hurl stones at her window.
Manure splatters glass.
The nurses are hiding something.

The shadow is a popish idol.
No, the shadow is the real Virgin Mary,
a visitation, a reincarnation,
a pill of light flickering in a dark country.

Laura Stanley

When I came to visit you at home

your dog's eyes always followed me around the room
showing me to my seat on your brown Parker Knoll,
shining, intensely black but somehow still

and I found that stillness reassuring
as we sat and talked about bunions and loneliness
and the irrelevant necessity of Viagra

because I was used to arriving at other visits anxious,
greeted by the muscled thud of a growling torso
launched against the door frame inside.

He's only being playful, the other owners used to say
between the snarls, the barks, the saliva dripped
like wet elastic in time to the beat of my fear.

But then there was your dog (good dog) —
so affectionate, so obedient, so still — a tribute
to your loving care and the almost obsolete art
of a Bow Road taxidermist.

Neil Douglas

Toyah Willcox and Robert Fripp cover 'Heroes' in lockdown on VE Day

He's thrashing the Bowie riff, that urgent beat
and she's singing the lyrics, holding up scrawled signs

that say 'Uncle Bill Fripp, who helped plan The Great Escape'
(which failed), and 'My Daddy stationed in the Med';

and I'm remembering a photo of my Dad and another
medical student, standing either side of a human head,

on a dissecting table; of my parents' refugee wedding
with Mum's hem coming down, and the grocery flowers,

still in their paper, to be put in a jam jar on an orange box
draped in cloth, in Prospect Rd, Swiss Cottage.

There are no pictures, as far as I know, of Dad lying
in a ward with only three walls, in Ware Sanatorium,

one lung collapsed, breathing fresh air, which was all
they had then, pre-Penicillin, for TB. 1941.

And I'm thinking the real heroes weren't those
who banked planes between flak, or fought

on the beaches, giving blood, toil, tears and sweat,
but maybe those who never took arms, who stood

in queues, ration book ready, for a can of pilchards,
though with Mum's accent, the woman kept giving her

peaches; she who wore her mother's best dress
to get married in, though it didn't fit any more,

because of all the biscuits she'd eaten, ravenous,
'in service' in Manchester; who at just twenty-three

had left that mother in Vienna, and would never
see or hear from her again; who 'charred' for the rich

of Hampstead Garden Suburb, because
Dad was so ill and not yet licenced to practise.

Sleeping in the Tube every night, under the sirens,
or stood crying on a crossroads in Hertford, looking

for somewhere to live away from bombs and smoke,
moving fourteen times in two years, digs to digs;

spending their lives in exile, neither belonging
to one place nor the other; who would lose

their clever, rootless son, plummeting drugged,
despairing, from a psychiatric ward window;

and who, for my sake, carried on living, working,
healing lung-choked miners, smokers, building

a home from the wreck of our family, telling me
all the stories, so I could be here, and write.

Veronica Zundel

Some data and a little insight

'There's no one here whose heart is still to break'
Roddy Lumsden after Po Chü-i

Behind textured glass you may see outlines
of what might be considered inmates.

Men come to this bar for company and quiet.
What they choose to discuss is not the point.

No-one's heart in that room is waiting
to be broken for the first time and the same

applies to those out here — the smokers
whose long spirits have begun to shrink

in a polite manner. Scars healing create
the same effect, by slow tightening

while an initial wound begins to dry.
In another place, to which reference

was made earlier, cardiographic studies
have shown how hearts not damaged

are so rare it is quite challenging to prove,
statistically speaking, that they exist at all.

Oliver Comins

The Spectacular Spinning Songbook Tour, 2011

After my brother dies young
a mixtape plays in my head

for two decades, as I imagine
him fixing anything that needs

to be fixed, providing Mum
with grandchildren, always there

in his turquoise 2 CV to give
me a lift. Whenever I find

a band that none of my friends
like, I know he would've gone

to see them with me, and when
one of the couples called up

to the stage at the Albert Hall
by Elvis Costello to choose

a song, reveals they're brother
and sister, there's a stranger

in the darkness next to me,
as Elvis and the band play

Everyday I Write the Book.

Louise Walker

The Goose Mother

The stubble alight in the dusk. Bitter smoke.
Overgrown ditches lead the road astray from our house.
Sepia. Dead grass. Cracked snails. Field mice fleeing.
My mother strides. She is as complete, immaculate
as a curling stone skimming across ice
or the first boulder to tumble onto the road
in a landslide. Her own person.
Wait for me: a crying bleat. The boulder turns.
Observes. *Wait for me*, it mocks. Then: *Hurry up.*
The geese cackle above, their arrow
pointing south. My mother's coat is goose down.
The geese she keeps have their wings clipped.
They will always have to wait:
they will never be their wild sisters.
She makes me shut the gate, collect their eggs,
make headdresses out of their feathers.

Zoë Green

Student Teacher

He arrived for just one term, ruddy-cheeked
and fresh out of Oxbridge. Miss Webb's scowl
was relegated to a seat
at the back of 6A, one heel dangling
from the ball of her arched foot, as he
leant corduroy-clad thighs on the desk in front of ours,
cupped the book of poems in his hands like a baby animal
and read to us the works of Keats and Clare
and Plath and Blake for the first time
whilst we crammed what he told us of their lives,
pencilling the romance of their lunacy
into the empty space around the text.

After school we swapped our streams of furtive imaginings
over MSN, mocked the plum mini skirt
Miss Webb turned up in one day, so short
David Robinson had to shield his eyes with his lever arch file.
We could tell she wanted him too, the trickle
of his voice on Thursday afternoons, his vowels
thrumming in our minds on the bus home
as the sky darkened and we became secretive
about sharing notes, burned for the rapture
of his inky scrawl on the tops of the essays
we offered up, warm from the printer
and straining just beyond the word count.

Penny Shutt

The Road

The immense dilapidation was without precedent on the road to Rajasthan. A policeman with a Mark-1 Lee Enfield, well worn by British use and his sergeant with massive black moustache and double-barrelled shotgun tested how far they could push us for a bribe, ignoring the two men riding a bicycle with a broken motor scooter on its cross bar or the fifteen men on a tricycle, or the man with thirty milk cans hanging from his bike.

Onwards into rag-bag chaos of cow dung and slime, colour and nobility and to the side calm from saried women squatting in line sickling wheat; stacks of drying cow dung pats stored to cook chapatis, boys hand-cranking presses crushing sugar cane and a naked child running into the road. A team of lorries heaving forward past a camel cart with chaff in bags of immense volume and no weight; two men pissing against a wall, a herd of goats and a painted elephant and a lorry coming in our direction in our gutter (if a gutter had existed) and holy men in bearded nakedness bathing in green rotten tanks under a red Hindu flag flying from the trees.

Cud-chewing cows lying on the highway, apologetic traffic avoiding them gently. Unused concrete pipes, a fantasy of sewage or irrigation now a resort for cobras and weeds and more cows with their bull, wandering across the road; Mr Singh my driver, inspired by his God Krishna, could predict exactly the path of the wandering cow, plotted his course accordingly.

A small town of shack-like shops, frontless and backless built of board in cow-laden mud; round groups of white clad men animated in circles whose speech could equal that of Aristotle; and a man with a bag of snakes and one with a bear chained and a woman carrying a load of bricks upon her head while men watch; nobody is killed; all accept that it need not change until they are reborn.

A tall man in stainless white with pink turban, then a host of camel carts, buses and lorries, tricycles, tractors and one donkey; school children with ironed shirts and striped ties and hand pumped water onto the back of buffalos and sex workers for lorry drivers at fifty rupees and temple and mosque side by side, where Rajasthani women veil their faces with the sari.

And a man carrying a hot smoking can of glue who goes from house to house fixing what is broken; then out of the town, scruffy youths play cricket by the road with pukka bat; a host of lorries stopped in line since ahead they know the Police are checking proof of local taxes paid, and more men pissing against a tree, and women rare or absent from the streets; a barber shaving faces by the road with homemade chair and mirror hung on a branch, and we move, sounding horns, all in slow motion; even the new pink limousine containing commercial Sikhs moves at the gluey pace of cows, buffalo and camel carts, donkeys, car transporters and oil tankers decorated with swastikas, but all flows like a shoal of interlocking fish. For hours it flows until one thousand sheep cross the National highway insensible to discordant honks.

We move around lorries rotting on their axles forward past more men pissing. Then, a round, delicate, deliciously restrained strong and peaceful white gift with river behind and grey reflecting marble in front, serene and perfect act of love in stone; Mogul mind and Hindu hand. Man is all these things: the sex worker awaiting her rupees, the Mogul Lord who built the Taj Mahal, and the pinkness, the pinkness, of the turban.

John Martin

Death Notice

Take three posters and nine pins
to hang news at three entrances.

Stick the pins firmly into the communal
board and feel the pricks on your skin.

Then go upstairs to the flat to get
what you can never get back.

Before you do stop at Janita's
to hand over a page – a personal touch.

After pour life into Babi's plants
as she once poured love into you.

Call up mum and find out what other
items you need to bring to the funeral.

Take three bags full of china that belonged
to your great grandmother Růženka.

We'll use them after the funeral for
the evening supper. They are the ones

with the purple flowers on them.
Pack them carefully, do not break even one!

I also grab a wedding photo. There is no
time for tears. It must be done.

Michael Klimeš

Grandad keeps pigeons and canaries

in the same cage. He has never hurt me. He probably could, so I follow,
skipping moss stuffed cracks in the concrete path,

the bolt is secured with wire, the padlock hangs
uncoupled. Green paint patchworks the rust. They flock

they flock to perch on the bloated head,
the bloated neck, the shiny sausage fist. They flock

and I look around this cage of shit, look at the face that frightens me.
Look at the perched, preening canaries, crooning pigeons

and he looks and asks and I say
yes, yes, I do like coming to see the birds.

Kathryn Anna Marshall

Petsamo

Before the Arctic Ocean Highway, there's me,
a farmer's wife, the blizzard that lasts six days

my enamelled milk jug on the table,
a bowl of pickled herring for dinner

my husband, who reads the Bible out, stumbles
on every word, asks me if I'm happy

Are you sure you've closed the gates?
his voice scraping like birch bark

my walk to the kitchen door, my prayer
for something like silence, the step

grandmother's voice as she sews my wedding clothes,
tells me what not to expect

down to sleet thick as darkness, that wind,
its pull, stronger than his arms

without snowshoes it takes three hours
to make twelve metres in that waist-deep white

instead of a timber fence, trees' bitter
fingers, numb hands, crisp tears

a crumb of bread, scraps of cloth
red like my woollen skirt

I should have used a rope, I should have
told him to stand and call my name

rusted nails from wooden soles,
a toothmarked femur, marrow sucked

before the thaw, there's my bed, the forest,
spooned warm around me, cold lamps of eyes

fox whips his tail,
ribbons across a studded sky

blinking down at something uncovered,
me, a farmer's wife, wishes granted

Morag Smith

Every time I come here, I wish that I could leave

After Jen Campbell

He brings my notes up on the screen, a few clicks
on his keyboard,

It appears, long and fragmented, and he scans:

    'Three months since you were last here, I see'

He says this every time, like he has no idea when he
last saw me, despite my being here every quarter

on a schedule he created. We talk briefly about my
pain levels since our last session, how many episodes
and what score I'd give each one.

    'Have you thought about coming off painkillers?'

I have. But now is not the right time.

He wants me to consider it again, stopping the drugs:

    'It gives your brain a chance to reset. For the medication
    to be at its most effective again. You should rethink.'

I tell him that I will, that as soon as I have time to
really prepare myself for 4 months of pain every day
I'll give him a call, he'll be the first to know.

He throws me a glance (this is not our first fight)
but backs away to a new topic

    [My lead neurologist who only has time to see me once
every two years, proposes these 'drug-free holidays' in
each of his letters to my GP. He has managed to condense
the idea of months of pain and uncertainty in two sentences,
when he remembers that I exist at all, with my hand covering
his notes, I don't think he could tell you my first name]

He scans my notes again before moving to the
procedure station, clean and cold, not unlike
his professional demeanour.

> [I never see anyone else waiting for this clinic. I've started
> to wonder if I'm some sort of lab experiment they conduct
> in secret]

I find it hard to sit still as he begins to prep the items, 3 bottles
of poison spread across 5 needles, beads of liquid rolling

down their points, mirroring the back of my neck, I start to breathe
heavily, like a boxer prepping for a big fight

He hasn't made eye contact with me this whole time, so he just
continues to measure doses, flicking gas bubbles out of the barrels,

he doesn't appreciate the stress of waiting, instead starts
telling me about his upcoming trip to Jordan, how he's been

looking forward to it all summer

> [I wonder if this is as close as he gets to wanting]

While he persists in telling me about what he is most looking forward to
he places a gloved hand on my forehead, measures finger spaces

to his desired location and begins the first of 48 injections, never
halting in his one-sided discussion as I flinch, bleed, pull away.

This always goes the same way, the finding of the first nerve, and the
follow through, tip to tip, forehead to shoulder, and repeat, 24 points
of paralysis along each vibrating highway.

When he's done, he turns away, takes off his gloves, and
places the needles carefully in a fluorescent yellow sharp's bin

and moves back to his PC, still no eye contact. A fresh pain
chart vomits from the printer, which he places a sticker with
the wrong name on and passes over to me. He hasn't looked at me

He says he hopes I have a nice summer, that he'll see me in 3 months
and starts to tap again on his keyboard. I pass the reception desk and two nurses

on my way out of the clinic before I reach the nearest bathroom, and stand
for a moment with my back against the door, trying to return my breathing to
normal

As I pass the line of mirrors on the way to the stall, I see streaks of blood
across my forehead, one trickling from a point behind my ear.

[He never wipes the blood away. I am contaminated tissue in this place
      left to roam the halls like I just saw battle]

Emily Fox

The Poets

Sharon Ashton's collaboration with Walsall New Art Gallery led to her first collection *Encounters with the Garman Ryan*, and her poems have appeared in *The Rialto*, *Mslexia*, *The Interpreter's House* and *The Alchemy Spoon*. Her novel *The Unravelling of Michael Gilchrist* was published in 2018, and she's recently completed another.

Oliver Comins recently moved back to Warwickshire after living in the Thames Valley for a long time. His poems are available in print and online and in short collections from Mandeville Press and Templar Poetry. A full-length collection (Oak Fish Island, 2018) was also published by Templar.

Ann Craig graduated from the Royal Scottish Academy, and is an Associate of the London College of Drama. She holds post graduates in Community Learning, and Philosophy. Born in Glasgow she still lives in Scotland. She is published in anthologies, and online. She has a poem on the Corbenic Path and recently performed at the Edinburgh Fringe for a BBC Radio Scotland recording of her work.

Sarah Drury is a poet, artist, and dreamer with an MA in creative writing. A former teacher, and Halle Choir soprano, she divides her time between writing, performing her poetry, home-educating, and painting in watercolours and acrylics. She was shortlisted for the Bridport Prize (2022) and Creative Future Writers' Award (2023).

Neil Douglas worked as a GP and Community Paediatrician in London's East End. His work has appeared in magazines and anthologies in the UK, North America and Hong Kong. He has recently graduated with an MA in Creative and Life Writing from Goldsmiths, University of London.

Emily Fox is a Bristol based poet, having just completed her Masters in Creative Writing at Oxford Brookes University under the tutelage of Mary Jean Chan. She has been shortlisted for the Bridport poetry prize, exhibited her work in Bristol, been published several anthologies, and is working towards a collection.

Zoë Green is a Scottish poet who lives and works in Thuringia. She has been published by *Under the Radar*, the *London Magazine*, and *Poetry Salzburg Review*. Her debut pamphlet, *Shadow Child*, will be published by Hedgehog Press later this year. X: @thetrampoet

Michael Klimeš is a financial journalist based in London. He has been published in *Alchemy Spoon*, *One Hand Clapping Magazine* and *Iota*. His pamphlet *Love Carries the Future* was shortlisted in the Full House Literary Magazine Digital Chapbook 2023 competition and longlisted in the *Alchemy Spoon* Pamphlet Competition 2023.

Kathryn Anna Marshall is a poet and writer from Shropshire. She has published in journals such as *Mslexia*, *Popshot Quarterly*, *Dreich* and *The Dawntreader* and online. Her first pamphlet *Dust*, written in memory of her brother, was published in 2022 and raised over £700 for mental health charities. Her series of poetry films can be found at kathrynannawrites.substack.com.

John Martin's 2004 collection, *The Origin of Loneliness* was followed by poems in *The London Magazine*, *Magma*, *The Lancet*, *Dreich*, *Trasna*, *Drawn to the Light*, *The Alchemy Spoon* and *Ink Drinkers* magazines. A former soldier, he studied philosophy before medicine and currently works as a doctor and scientist in Europe and the US.

Julie Runacres is recently retired and based in Leicestershire, having taught English at schools in Oxford and West London. Long-listed in the 2023 National Poetry Competition, her poems have appeared in journals including *14 Magazine* and *Long Poem Magazine* in the UK, and *Twyckenham Notes* in the US.

Penny Shutt is a poet and psychiatrist working in Edinburgh. Her poems have appeared in the Hippocrates prize anthologies and NHS *These are the Hands* anthology. She is a Hawthornden fellow and read with Hollie McNish at 2022's McLellan prize.

Morag Smith's poetry has won or been shortlisted for numerous prizes and published in magazines and anthologies, including *Poetry Ireland Review*, *The Scotsman* and *Gutter*. Her pamphlet, *Background Noises*, about the rewilding and human history of the semi-derelict Dykebar Psychiatric Hospital near Paisley, Scotland, is available at *redsquirrelpress.com*

Laura Stanley completed her Creative Writing MA at the University of Birmingham. Her heresy has been published in *Anthropocene*, *bath magg*, *Magma*, *The Interpreter's House*, *The Alchemy Spoon*, *The New Welsh Review*, *Blackbox Manifold* and by the Young Poets Network.

Louise Walker is a retired English teacher. Her poems have appeared in several anthologies and journals. Highly Commended in the Frosted Fire Firsts Award (2022), she won 3rd prize in the Ironbridge Poetry Competition (2023). Commissions include Bampton Classical Opera and Gill Wing Jewellery for their showcase 'Poetry in Ocean'.

Judith Wozniak has an MA in Writing Poetry. Her poems have appeared in *The Alchemy Spoon, Fenland Poetry Journal, The Frogmore Papers, London Grip* and *Ink Sweat & Tears*. She won first prize in the Hippocrates Competition 2020. Her pamphlet, *Patient Watching*, was published by The Hedgehog Press in 2022.

Veronica Zundel has had poems published in *Magma*, *Snakeskin*, *Ekphrastic Review* and several anthologies and has won the Barnet and Cruse Lines prizes. Her poetry has featured on Radios 2 and 4 and in an Open University foundation course. She has an MA in Writing Poetry from the Poetry School.

Senior Copy Editor Sara Levy

Proof-reader Adam Lampert

www.clayhangerpress.co.uk

www.ingramcontent.com/pod-product-compliance
Lightning Source LLC
Chambersburg PA
CBHW052209110526
44591CB00012B/2147